50 Chilean Recipes for Home

By: Kelly Johnson

Table of Contents

- Empanadas de Pino
- Pastel de Choclo
- Cazuela de Pollo
- Asado al Palo
- Completo (Chilean Hot Dog)
- Pebre
- Chorrillana
- Porotos Granados
- Charquicán
- Chicha
- Sopaipillas
- Lomo a lo Pobre
- Parrillada
- Chupes de Jaiba
- Pisco Sour
- Calzones Rotos
- Humitas
- Machas a la Parmesana
- Curanto
- Leche Asada
- Sopa de Mariscos
- Tomatican
- Sopa de Porotos
- Pan Amasado
- Milcaos
- Arrollado Huaso
- Calapurca
- Alfajores
- Estofado de Pollo
- Pastel de Papas
- Kuchen
- Pastel de Jaiba
- Sopa de Zapallo
- Curanto en Olla
- Pernil de Cerdo

- Sopa de Lentejas
- Humitas en Olla
- Chapalele
- Chilenitos
- Cola de Mono
- Chupe de Locos
- Chirimoya Sour
- Machas a la Parmesana
- Cochayuyo en Ensalada
- Sopa de Zapallo Italiano
- Sopa de Tortilla
- Charquican de Chuchoca
- Pollo Arvejado
- Sopa de Champiñones
- Berlín

Empanadas de Pino

Ingredients:

For the dough:

- 3 cups all-purpose flour
- 1/2 cup (1 stick) unsalted butter, chilled and cut into small cubes
- 1/2 cup water
- 1 teaspoon salt
- 1 egg, beaten (for egg wash)

For the filling:

- 1 lb ground beef
- 1 onion, finely chopped
- 2 cloves garlic, minced
- 2 hard-boiled eggs, chopped
- 1/2 cup pitted black olives, chopped
- 1/4 cup raisins (optional)
- 1 teaspoon ground cumin
- 1 teaspoon paprika
- 1/2 teaspoon ground black pepper
- Salt, to taste
- Cooking oil

Instructions:

1. In a large mixing bowl, combine the flour and salt. Add the chilled butter cubes and use your fingers to rub the butter into the flour until the mixture resembles coarse crumbs.
2. Gradually add the water to the flour mixture, mixing until a dough forms. Knead the dough on a lightly floured surface until smooth. Wrap the dough in plastic wrap and refrigerate for at least 30 minutes.

3. While the dough is chilling, prepare the filling. Heat a tablespoon of cooking oil in a skillet over medium heat. Add the chopped onion and garlic and cook until softened.
4. Add the ground beef to the skillet and cook until browned, breaking it up with a spoon as it cooks. Drain any excess fat from the skillet.
5. Stir in the chopped hard-boiled eggs, chopped olives, and raisins (if using). Season the filling with ground cumin, paprika, black pepper, and salt to taste. Cook for a few more minutes until the flavors are well combined. Remove the skillet from the heat and let the filling cool slightly.
6. Preheat your oven to 375°F (190°C). Line a baking sheet with parchment paper.
7. On a lightly floured surface, roll out the chilled dough to about 1/8 inch thickness. Use a round cutter or a small bowl to cut out circles of dough.
8. Place a spoonful of the beef filling in the center of each dough circle. Fold the dough over the filling to create a half-moon shape, then crimp the edges to seal. You can use a fork to press the edges together or twist and fold them to create a decorative edge.
9. Transfer the assembled empanadas to the prepared baking sheet. Brush the tops of the empanadas with beaten egg for a golden finish.
10. Bake the empanadas in the preheated oven for 20-25 minutes, or until they are golden brown and crispy.
11. Remove the empanadas from the oven and let them cool slightly before serving.

Enjoy your homemade Empanadas de Pino as a delicious and satisfying meal or snack!

Pastel de Choclo

Ingredients:

For the filling:

- 1 lb ground beef
- 1 onion, chopped
- 2 cloves garlic, minced
- 1 red bell pepper, chopped
- 1 tablespoon ground cumin
- 1 teaspoon paprika
- Salt and pepper to taste
- 1/2 cup black olives, pitted and sliced
- 4 hard-boiled eggs, sliced
- 1/2 cup raisins (optional)

For the corn topping (Choclo):

- 6 ears of corn, kernels removed (or 4 cups of frozen corn kernels)
- 1 cup milk
- 2 tablespoons butter
- 1 tablespoon sugar
- Salt to taste

For assembling:

- 1 tablespoon vegetable oil
- 1 tablespoon powdered sugar (for dusting)
- Fresh basil leaves (for garnish, optional)

Instructions:

1. Preheat your oven to 375°F (190°C).

2. In a large skillet, heat the vegetable oil over medium heat. Add the chopped onion and garlic, and cook until softened.
3. Add the ground beef to the skillet and cook until browned, breaking it up with a spoon as it cooks.
4. Stir in the chopped red bell pepper, ground cumin, paprika, salt, and pepper. Cook for a few more minutes until the bell pepper is tender.
5. Remove the skillet from the heat and stir in the sliced black olives and raisins (if using). Set the filling aside.
6. In a blender or food processor, blend the corn kernels with milk until smooth.
7. Pour the corn mixture into a saucepan and add the butter, sugar, and salt. Cook over medium heat, stirring constantly, until the mixture thickens and resembles a thick porridge. Remove from heat and set aside.
8. To assemble the Pastel de Choclo, grease a large baking dish with butter or oil. Spread half of the corn mixture evenly over the bottom of the dish.
9. Spoon the beef filling over the corn layer, spreading it out evenly.
10. Arrange the sliced hard-boiled eggs over the beef filling in an even layer.
11. Cover the filling with the remaining corn mixture, spreading it out evenly with a spatula.
12. Bake the Pastel de Choclo in the preheated oven for 30-40 minutes, or until the top is golden brown and the filling is heated through.
13. Remove the Pastel de Choclo from the oven and let it cool slightly before serving.
14. To serve, sprinkle the powdered sugar over the top of the Pastel de Choclo and garnish with fresh basil leaves if desired.

Enjoy this delicious and comforting Chilean dish with your family and friends!

Cazuela de Pollo

Ingredients:

- 2 lbs chicken pieces (such as thighs, drumsticks, or breasts), bone-in and skin-on
- 2 tablespoons vegetable oil
- 1 onion, chopped
- 2 cloves garlic, minced
- 2 carrots, peeled and diced
- 2 potatoes, peeled and diced
- 1 bell pepper, diced
- 1 cup green beans, trimmed and cut into 1-inch pieces
- 1 cup corn kernels (fresh or frozen)
- 1 cup pumpkin or squash, peeled and diced
- 1/2 cup rice
- 6 cups chicken broth
- 1 teaspoon ground cumin
- 1 teaspoon paprika
- 1/2 teaspoon dried oregano
- Salt and pepper to taste
- Fresh cilantro or parsley, chopped (for garnish)

Instructions:

1. Season the chicken pieces with salt and pepper.
2. In a large pot or Dutch oven, heat the vegetable oil over medium heat. Add the chicken pieces and cook until browned on all sides. Remove the chicken from the pot and set aside.
3. In the same pot, add the chopped onion and garlic. Cook until softened and fragrant.
4. Add the diced carrots, potatoes, bell pepper, green beans, corn kernels, and pumpkin or squash to the pot. Cook for a few minutes until the vegetables start to soften.
5. Return the chicken pieces to the pot. Add the rice, chicken broth, ground cumin, paprika, dried oregano, and additional salt and pepper to taste. Stir to combine.

6. Bring the cazuela to a boil, then reduce the heat to low. Cover and simmer for about 30-40 minutes, or until the chicken is cooked through and the vegetables are tender.
7. Taste and adjust the seasoning if needed. If the stew is too thick, you can add more chicken broth or water.
8. Serve the cazuela de pollo hot, garnished with chopped cilantro or parsley.

Enjoy this comforting and hearty Chilean chicken stew with your favorite bread or rice on the side!

Asado al Palo

Ingredients:

- 4-6 lbs beef or lamb (cuts like ribs, sirloin, or flank steak)
- Salt and pepper to taste
- Wooden skewers or "palos"
- Optional: Chimichurri sauce or salsa criolla for serving

Instructions:

1. Prepare your grill or open fire pit for cooking. If you're using wood skewers, soak them in water for at least 30 minutes to prevent them from burning.
2. Season the meat generously with salt and pepper on all sides.
3. Thread the seasoned meat onto the wooden skewers, making sure to leave some space between each piece to allow for even cooking.
4. Once the fire is hot and the flames have died down, place the skewers of meat over the grill or fire pit, positioning them so they are slightly angled towards the flames.
5. Cook the meat slowly, rotating the skewers occasionally to ensure that all sides are evenly cooked. The cooking time will vary depending on the type and thickness of the meat, but it typically takes 1-2 hours for the meat to cook through and develop a nice charred exterior.
6. As the meat cooks, baste it occasionally with any accumulated juices or marinade to keep it moist and flavorful.
7. Once the meat is cooked to your desired level of doneness, remove the skewers from the grill or fire pit and let them rest for a few minutes before serving.
8. Serve the Asado al Palo hot, either straight from the skewers or sliced and plated. Accompany it with chimichurri sauce or salsa criolla for extra flavor.

Enjoy the smoky and succulent flavors of Asado al Palo, a beloved Chilean barbecue tradition!

Completo (Chilean Hot Dog)

Ingredients:

- 4 hot dog buns
- 4 beef or pork hot dogs
- 1 ripe avocado, sliced
- 1/2 cup sauerkraut
- 1/2 cup diced tomatoes
- 1/4 cup diced onions
- 1/4 cup mayonnaise
- 1/4 cup ketchup
- 1/4 cup yellow mustard
- Optional: chopped cilantro or parsley for garnish
- Optional: chopped pickles or jalapeños for extra flavor

Instructions:

1. Heat a grill or skillet over medium heat. Cook the hot dogs until they are heated through and have grill marks, about 5-7 minutes.
2. While the hot dogs are cooking, lightly toast the hot dog buns until golden brown.
3. Place a hot dog in each bun.
4. Top each Completo with slices of ripe avocado.
5. Add a spoonful of sauerkraut to each hot dog.
6. Sprinkle diced tomatoes and onions over the top of each Completo.
7. In a small bowl, mix together the mayonnaise, ketchup, and yellow mustard to make a sauce.
8. Drizzle the sauce over the Completo.
9. Garnish with chopped cilantro or parsley, and add chopped pickles or jalapeños if desired.
10. Serve the Completo immediately, and enjoy the unique flavors of this Chilean street food!

Feel free to customize your Completo with your favorite toppings or condiments to suit your taste preferences.

Pebre

Ingredients:

- 2 medium tomatoes, finely chopped
- 1/2 cup finely chopped onion
- 1/4 cup chopped fresh cilantro
- 2 cloves garlic, minced
- 1-2 hot peppers (such as jalapeño or serrano), finely chopped (adjust according to your spice preference)
- 2 tablespoons olive oil
- 2 tablespoons white vinegar or freshly squeezed lemon juice
- Salt to taste

Instructions:

1. In a mixing bowl, combine the chopped tomatoes, onion, cilantro, minced garlic, and chopped hot peppers.
2. Drizzle the olive oil and vinegar (or lemon juice) over the mixture.
3. Season with salt to taste.
4. Stir all the ingredients together until well combined.
5. Cover the bowl with plastic wrap or a lid and refrigerate for at least 30 minutes to allow the flavors to meld together.
6. Taste and adjust the seasoning if needed, adding more salt or vinegar according to your preference.
7. Serve Pebre as a condiment alongside grilled meats, empanadas, sandwiches, or any other dishes where you want to add a burst of freshness and spice.
8. Store any leftover Pebre in an airtight container in the refrigerator for up to 3-4 days.

Enjoy the vibrant flavors of homemade Pebre as a versatile and delicious addition to your meals! Adjust the amount of hot peppers according to your desired level of spiciness.

Chorrillana

Ingredients:

- 1 lb French fries (homemade or store-bought)
- 1 onion, thinly sliced
- 1 lb beef or pork, thinly sliced
- 4 eggs
- Salt and pepper to taste
- Cooking oil

Optional toppings:

- Sausage slices
- Grated cheese
- Chopped parsley or green onions for garnish
- Salsa or hot sauce for serving

Instructions:

1. Prepare the French fries according to your preferred method. You can fry them, bake them in the oven, or use frozen fries that have been cooked according to the package instructions.
2. While the fries are cooking, heat a tablespoon of cooking oil in a skillet over medium heat. Add the sliced onions and cook until soft and caramelized, about 5-7 minutes. Remove the onions from the skillet and set aside.
3. In the same skillet, add another tablespoon of oil if needed, then add the sliced beef or pork. Season with salt and pepper to taste and cook until browned and cooked through, about 5-7 minutes. Remove the meat from the skillet and set aside.
4. In the same skillet, crack the eggs and scramble them until cooked to your liking. Season with salt and pepper to taste.
5. Once all the components are ready, assemble the Chorrillana on a large serving platter or individual plates. Start with a layer of French fries, then top with the sautéed onions, cooked meat, and scrambled eggs.
6. If desired, add additional toppings such as sausage slices or grated cheese.
7. Garnish with chopped parsley or green onions for a pop of color and freshness.

8. Serve the Chorrillana hot, accompanied by salsa or hot sauce on the side for extra flavor.

Enjoy this hearty and indulgent dish that's perfect for sharing with friends and family! Feel free to customize the toppings according to your taste preferences.

Porotos Granados

Ingredients:

- 2 cups fresh cranberry beans (or dried beans, soaked overnight)
- 2 cups diced squash (such as butternut or kabocha)
- 1 cup fresh corn kernels (or frozen corn)
- 1 onion, chopped
- 2 cloves garlic, minced
- 1 red bell pepper, diced
- 2 tomatoes, diced
- 1 tablespoon paprika
- 1 teaspoon ground cumin
- 1 teaspoon dried oregano
- Salt and pepper to taste
- Fresh basil leaves, chopped, for garnish
- Olive oil
- Optional: diced pumpkin or potatoes for added heartiness

Instructions:

1. If using dried beans, drain and rinse them after soaking overnight. If using fresh cranberry beans, shell them and rinse them thoroughly.
2. In a large pot, heat a drizzle of olive oil over medium heat. Add the chopped onion and garlic and cook until softened and fragrant.
3. Add the diced squash, red bell pepper, and tomatoes to the pot. Cook for a few minutes until the vegetables start to soften.
4. Add the fresh cranberry beans (or soaked dried beans) to the pot, along with the paprika, ground cumin, dried oregano, salt, and pepper. Stir to combine.
5. Add enough water to the pot to cover the ingredients by about an inch. Bring the mixture to a boil, then reduce the heat to low and let it simmer gently, uncovered, for about 30 minutes to an hour, or until the beans are tender.
6. About halfway through the cooking time, add the fresh corn kernels (or frozen corn) to the pot and continue cooking until all the vegetables and beans are tender.
7. Taste and adjust the seasoning if needed, adding more salt and pepper to taste.
8. Once the Porotos Granados is cooked and the flavors have melded together, remove the pot from the heat.

9. Serve the Porotos Granados hot, garnished with chopped fresh basil leaves for a burst of freshness.

Enjoy this delicious and nutritious Chilean stew as a comforting meal on its own or with a slice of crusty bread for dipping!

Charquicán

Ingredients:

- 4 large potatoes, peeled and diced
- 1 lb beef or pork, diced (you can also use leftover cooked meat)
- 1 onion, chopped
- 2 cloves garlic, minced
- 2 carrots, diced
- 1 cup frozen corn kernels
- 1 cup frozen peas
- 1 red bell pepper, diced
- 1 teaspoon ground cumin
- 1 teaspoon paprika
- Salt and pepper to taste
- Vegetable oil
- Fresh cilantro or parsley, chopped, for garnish (optional)

Instructions:

1. Place the diced potatoes in a large pot and cover them with water. Bring the water to a boil, then reduce the heat to medium-low and simmer the potatoes until they are fork-tender, about 15-20 minutes. Drain the potatoes and set them aside.
2. In a large skillet, heat a drizzle of vegetable oil over medium heat. Add the diced meat to the skillet and cook until browned on all sides. Remove the meat from the skillet and set it aside.
3. In the same skillet, add a little more oil if needed, then add the chopped onion and garlic. Sauté until the onion is soft and translucent, about 5 minutes.
4. Add the diced carrots, bell pepper, frozen corn, and frozen peas to the skillet. Cook for a few more minutes until the vegetables start to soften.
5. Return the cooked meat to the skillet. Season the mixture with ground cumin, paprika, salt, and pepper to taste. Stir to combine.
6. Add the cooked potatoes to the skillet and use a potato masher to mash them into the meat and vegetable mixture, creating a rough mash.
7. Continue cooking the Charquicán for a few more minutes until everything is heated through and well combined.
8. Taste and adjust the seasoning if needed, adding more salt and pepper to taste.

9. Serve the Charquicán hot, garnished with chopped fresh cilantro or parsley if desired.

Enjoy this comforting and flavorful Chilean dish as a satisfying meal on its own or accompanied by a simple salad or crusty bread!

Chicha

Ingredients:

- 2 lbs dried maize (yellow or white corn), preferably Jora corn if available
- 4 quarts water
- 1 cinnamon stick
- 3 cloves
- 1 pineapple, peeled and chopped
- 1 cup brown sugar (or to taste)
- 1/4 cup fresh lemon or lime juice
- Optional: additional spices such as cloves, allspice, or star anise

Instructions:

1. Rinse the dried maize thoroughly under cold water to remove any dirt or debris.
2. In a large pot, combine the maize with the water, cinnamon stick, and cloves. Bring the mixture to a boil over medium-high heat, then reduce the heat to low and let it simmer for 2-3 hours, stirring occasionally. The maize should become soft and start to break down.
3. Once the maize is soft, remove the pot from the heat and let it cool to room temperature.
4. Once cooled, strain the liquid through a fine-mesh sieve or cheesecloth into a clean container, discarding the solids. You should be left with a milky liquid known as "chicha."
5. Add the chopped pineapple to the chicha, along with the brown sugar and fresh lemon or lime juice. Stir until the sugar is dissolved.
6. Cover the container with a clean cloth or lid and let it sit at room temperature for 1-2 days to ferment. The fermentation time may vary depending on the temperature and desired level of fermentation. During fermentation, the chicha will develop a slightly sour taste and a fizzy texture.
7. Once fermented to your liking, refrigerate the chicha to stop the fermentation process. Serve cold over ice, and enjoy responsibly!

Note: Chicha de Jora can be a mildly alcoholic beverage due to the fermentation process. It's important to monitor the fermentation time and consume it responsibly, especially if serving to children or individuals who avoid alcohol. Adjust the sugar and lemon/lime juice to taste, as the sweetness and acidity can vary depending on personal preference and the ripeness of the pineapple.

Sopaipillas

Ingredients:

- 2 cups all-purpose flour
- 1 cup cooked and mashed pumpkin or squash (canned pumpkin puree can also be used)
- 1 teaspoon baking powder
- 1/2 teaspoon salt
- 1 tablespoon granulated sugar
- Water, as needed
- Vegetable oil, for frying
- Optional: ground cinnamon and powdered sugar for dusting

Instructions:

1. In a large mixing bowl, combine the flour, mashed pumpkin or squash, baking powder, salt, and sugar. Mix until well combined.
2. Gradually add water to the mixture, a little at a time, and knead the dough until it comes together and is smooth and elastic. The dough should be soft but not sticky. Add more flour if necessary to achieve the right consistency.
3. Cover the dough with a clean kitchen towel or plastic wrap and let it rest for about 15-20 minutes.
4. Meanwhile, heat vegetable oil in a deep fryer or large skillet to 350°F (175°C).
5. Once the dough has rested, divide it into smaller portions and roll each portion into a ball. On a lightly floured surface, flatten each ball into a thin disc, about 1/4 inch thick.
6. Use a sharp knife or pastry cutter to cut each disc into desired shapes, such as circles or squares.
7. Carefully place the sopaipillas into the hot oil, frying them in batches to avoid overcrowding the pan. Fry until golden brown and puffed up, about 2-3 minutes per side.
8. Use a slotted spoon to transfer the fried sopaipillas to a paper towel-lined plate to drain excess oil.
9. If desired, dust the sopaipillas with a mixture of ground cinnamon and powdered sugar while they are still warm.
10. Serve the sopaipillas warm and enjoy them as a delicious snack or dessert!

These sopaipillas are best enjoyed fresh and warm, but you can also store any leftovers in an airtight container at room temperature for a day or two. Simply reheat them in the oven or microwave before serving.

Lomo a lo Pobre

Ingredients:

- 4 beef sirloin steaks, about 1/2 inch thick
- Salt and pepper to taste
- 4 large potatoes, peeled and cut into thick fries
- Vegetable oil for frying
- 2 large onions, thinly sliced
- 4 eggs
- Cooked rice, for serving (optional)
- Fresh parsley or cilantro, chopped, for garnish (optional)

Instructions:

1. Season the beef steaks generously with salt and pepper on both sides.
2. In a large skillet, heat a drizzle of vegetable oil over medium-high heat. Add the sliced onions and cook, stirring occasionally, until they are soft and caramelized, about 15-20 minutes. Remove the onions from the skillet and set them aside.
3. In the same skillet, add more oil if needed, then add the potato fries in batches. Fry them until they are golden brown and crispy, about 5-7 minutes per batch. Remove the fries from the skillet and drain them on paper towels.
4. Keep the fries warm in the oven while you cook the steaks and eggs.
5. In the same skillet, cook the beef steaks to your desired level of doneness, about 3-4 minutes per side for medium-rare. Remove the steaks from the skillet and let them rest for a few minutes.
6. While the steaks are resting, fry the eggs in the same skillet until the whites are set but the yolks are still runny, about 3-4 minutes.
7. To serve, place a steak on each plate and top it with a generous portion of caramelized onions. Arrange a mound of crispy fries next to the steak, and top the fries with a fried egg.
8. Garnish with chopped parsley or cilantro if desired, and serve immediately, accompanied by cooked rice if desired.

Enjoy this indulgent and satisfying Chilean dish with your favorite sides and a glass of red wine for a truly comforting meal!

Parrillada

Ingredients:

- Assorted meats such as beef steaks, pork chops, sausages, chicken thighs, and ribs
- Salt and pepper to taste
- Marinade or seasoning blend of your choice (optional)
- Vegetable oil for grilling
- Chimichurri sauce or salsa criolla for serving (optional)
- Side dishes such as grilled vegetables, roasted potatoes, or salad

Instructions:

1. Prepare your grill for high heat cooking. If using a charcoal grill, light the charcoal and let it burn until the coals are glowing red-hot. If using a gas grill, preheat the grill to high heat.
2. Season the assorted meats with salt, pepper, and any additional marinade or seasoning blend of your choice. Allow the meat to marinate for at least 30 minutes to allow the flavors to penetrate.
3. Once the grill is hot, lightly oil the grates to prevent the meat from sticking.
4. Place the seasoned meats on the grill, arranging them so that there is space between each piece to allow for even cooking.
5. Grill the meats, turning them occasionally, until they are cooked to your desired level of doneness. The cooking time will vary depending on the type and thickness of the meat.
6. As the meats cook, you can also grill any additional side dishes such as vegetables or potatoes.
7. Once the meats are cooked, remove them from the grill and transfer them to a serving platter.
8. Serve the Parrillada hot, accompanied by chimichurri sauce or salsa criolla if desired, along with your choice of side dishes.
9. Enjoy the Parrillada with friends and family, and savor the delicious flavors of grilled meats and accompaniments!

Feel free to customize your Parrillada with your favorite meats and side dishes, and adjust the seasoning and sauces according to your taste preferences.

Chupes de Jaiba

Ingredients:

- 1 lb fresh or canned crabmeat (you can also use whole crabs and extract the meat)
- 2 tablespoons vegetable oil
- 1 onion, finely chopped
- 2 cloves garlic, minced
- 2 tomatoes, diced
- 1 teaspoon paprika
- 1/2 teaspoon ground cumin
- 4 cups fish or vegetable broth
- 2 cups diced potatoes
- 1 cup fresh or frozen corn kernels
- 1 cup peas (fresh or frozen)
- 1 cup heavy cream
- Salt and pepper to taste
- Fresh cilantro or parsley, chopped, for garnish (optional)
- Lemon wedges, for serving

Instructions:

1. If using whole crabs, clean them thoroughly and extract the meat. Discard the shells and set the crabmeat aside.
2. In a large pot, heat the vegetable oil over medium heat. Add the chopped onion and garlic and sauté until softened and fragrant, about 5 minutes.
3. Add the diced tomatoes, paprika, and ground cumin to the pot. Cook for another 5 minutes, stirring occasionally, until the tomatoes have softened and released their juices.
4. Pour the fish or vegetable broth into the pot and bring the mixture to a simmer.
5. Add the diced potatoes to the pot and simmer for about 10 minutes, or until the potatoes are just tender.
6. Stir in the corn kernels, peas, and crabmeat. Simmer for another 5 minutes, or until the crabmeat is heated through and the vegetables are tender.
7. Pour in the heavy cream and stir to combine. Season the stew with salt and pepper to taste.

8. Continue to simmer the Chupes de Jaiba for another 5 minutes to allow the flavors to meld together.
9. Once the stew is ready, remove it from the heat and ladle it into serving bowls.
10. Garnish each bowl with chopped fresh cilantro or parsley, if desired, and serve hot with lemon wedges on the side.
11. Enjoy the delicious and comforting flavors of Chupes de Jaiba with crusty bread or rice on the side!

Feel free to adjust the ingredients and seasonings according to your taste preferences, and add extra vegetables or seafood if desired.

Pisco Sour

Ingredients:

- 2 oz Pisco
- 1 oz fresh lime juice
- 3/4 oz simple syrup (equal parts water and sugar)
- 1 egg white
- Angostura bitters, for garnish
- Ice cubes

Instructions:

1. In a cocktail shaker, combine the Pisco, fresh lime juice, simple syrup, and egg white.
2. Add a handful of ice cubes to the shaker.
3. Shake the ingredients vigorously for about 15-20 seconds to chill the mixture and create a frothy texture.
4. Strain the cocktail into a chilled glass filled with ice.
5. Garnish the Pisco Sour with a few drops of Angostura bitters on top.
6. Serve immediately and enjoy!

Note: If you're concerned about using raw egg white, you can substitute it with pasteurized egg white or omit it altogether. However, the egg white adds a creamy texture and frothiness to the cocktail that is characteristic of a traditional Pisco Sour.

Feel free to adjust the proportions of Pisco, lime juice, and simple syrup to suit your taste preferences. Some people prefer a more tart or sweeter version of the cocktail. Additionally, you can experiment with different types of Pisco to create variations of the classic Pisco Sour. Cheers!

Calzones Rotos

Ingredients:

- 2 cups all-purpose flour
- 1/4 cup granulated sugar
- 1/4 teaspoon salt
- 2 teaspoons baking powder
- 2 large eggs
- 1/4 cup milk
- 2 tablespoons butter, melted
- Vegetable oil, for frying
- Powdered sugar, for dusting

Instructions:

1. In a large mixing bowl, combine the flour, sugar, salt, and baking powder.
2. In a separate bowl, whisk together the eggs, milk, and melted butter until well combined.
3. Pour the wet ingredients into the dry ingredients and mix until a dough forms. If the dough is too dry, you can add a little more milk, a tablespoon at a time, until it comes together.
4. Turn the dough out onto a lightly floured surface and knead it gently for a few minutes until smooth.
5. Divide the dough into smaller portions and roll each portion into a thin circle, about 1/4 inch thick.
6. Use a sharp knife or pizza cutter to cut each circle of dough into smaller pieces, about 2 inches wide.
7. Heat vegetable oil in a deep fryer or large skillet to 350°F (175°C).
8. Carefully place a few pieces of dough into the hot oil, being careful not to overcrowd the pan. Fry the dough pieces until they are golden brown and crispy, about 2-3 minutes per side.
9. Use a slotted spoon to transfer the fried dough to a paper towel-lined plate to drain any excess oil.
10. Repeat the frying process with the remaining dough pieces.
11. Once all the Calzones Rotos are fried, dust them generously with powdered sugar while they are still warm.

12. Serve the Calzones Rotos immediately, and enjoy them as a sweet and crispy treat!

These Calzones Rotos are best enjoyed fresh and warm, but you can also store any leftovers in an airtight container at room temperature for a day or two. Simply reheat them in the oven or microwave before serving.

Humitas

Ingredients:

- 6 ears fresh corn, husked and kernels removed (about 4 cups)
- 1 onion, finely chopped
- 2 tablespoons vegetable oil
- 1/2 cup milk
- 1/4 cup cornmeal or masa harina
- 1/4 cup grated cheese (such as queso fresco or mozzarella)
- 1 teaspoon baking powder
- Salt and pepper to taste
- Corn husks, soaked in warm water for at least 30 minutes

Instructions:

1. In a large skillet, heat the vegetable oil over medium heat. Add the chopped onion and cook until softened and translucent, about 5 minutes.
2. In a food processor or blender, puree half of the corn kernels until smooth. Transfer the pureed corn to a large mixing bowl.
3. Add the remaining corn kernels to the bowl with the pureed corn.
4. Add the cooked onion, milk, cornmeal or masa harina, grated cheese, baking powder, salt, and pepper to the bowl with the corn mixture. Stir until well combined.
5. Take a corn husk and place about 1/4 cup of the corn mixture in the center of the husk.
6. Fold the sides of the husk over the filling, then fold up the bottom of the husk to enclose the filling completely. Secure the packet with kitchen twine if needed.
7. Repeat the process with the remaining corn mixture and corn husks.
8. Fill a large pot with a few inches of water and bring it to a boil. Place a steamer basket or colander in the pot, making sure the water does not touch the bottom of the basket.
9. Arrange the humitas in the steamer basket or colander, cover the pot with a lid, and steam the humitas for about 45-60 minutes, or until the filling is firm and cooked through.
10. Remove the humitas from the steamer and let them cool for a few minutes before serving.

11. To serve, unwrap the corn husks and enjoy the humitas warm as a delicious and comforting snack or side dish.

Feel free to customize the filling with additional ingredients such as chopped peppers, herbs, or spices, according to your taste preferences. Enjoy your homemade humitas!

Machas a la Parmesana

Ingredients:

- 12-16 fresh machas (razor clams), cleaned and shelled
- 1/2 cup grated Parmesan cheese
- 4 tablespoons butter, softened
- 2 cloves garlic, minced
- 1/4 cup breadcrumbs
- 2 tablespoons chopped fresh parsley
- Salt and pepper to taste
- Lemon wedges, for serving

Instructions:

1. Preheat your oven to 400°F (200°C). Lightly grease a baking dish or a baking sheet with cooking spray or butter.
2. Arrange the cleaned and shelled machas in a single layer in the prepared baking dish or baking sheet.
3. In a small bowl, combine the grated Parmesan cheese, softened butter, minced garlic, breadcrumbs, chopped fresh parsley, salt, and pepper. Mix until well combined.
4. Spoon the Parmesan mixture evenly over the machas, covering each one with a generous amount of topping.
5. Place the baking dish or baking sheet in the preheated oven and bake the Machas a la Parmesana for about 8-10 minutes, or until the topping is golden brown and bubbly.
6. Remove the dish from the oven and let the Machas a la Parmesana cool for a few minutes before serving.
7. Serve the Machas a la Parmesana hot, garnished with lemon wedges on the side for squeezing over the clams.
8. Enjoy the delicious flavors of the cheesy, garlicky topping paired with the tender and flavorful machas as a tasty appetizer or snack!

Feel free to adjust the ingredients and seasonings according to your taste preferences.

You can also add a splash of white wine or lemon juice to the Parmesan mixture for extra flavor. Serve the Machas a la Parmesana with crusty bread or a side salad for a complete meal. Enjoy!

Curanto

Ingredients:

- Assorted meats such as beef, pork, chicken, and/or lamb
- Assorted seafood such as clams, mussels, shrimp, and/or fish fillets
- Potatoes, preferably small waxy potatoes
- Sweet potatoes or yams
- Corn on the cob
- Sausages, such as chorizo or longaniza
- Fresh herbs, such as cilantro or parsley
- Banana leaves or foil, for wrapping
- Rocks or stones for heating
- Large pit or hole in the ground, lined with stones

Instructions:

1. Start by heating the rocks or stones in the pit or hole until they are red-hot.
2. While the rocks are heating, prepare the meats, seafood, potatoes, and vegetables. Cut them into manageable pieces and season them as desired with salt, pepper, and any other spices or herbs you like.
3. Once the rocks are hot, place a layer of banana leaves or foil on top of them to prevent the food from burning.
4. Arrange the meats, seafood, potatoes, sweet potatoes, corn, and sausages on top of the banana leaves or foil in layers, making sure everything is evenly distributed.
5. Cover the ingredients with more banana leaves or foil to create a sealed packet.
6. Use dirt or sand to cover the entire pit or hole and seal in the heat.
7. Let the Curanto cook underground for several hours, allowing the flavors to meld together and the meats and seafood to become tender and flavorful.
8. After a few hours, carefully uncover the pit or hole and remove the banana leaves or foil packet.
9. Transfer the cooked Curanto to serving platters and garnish with fresh herbs.
10. Serve the Curanto hot, accompanied by traditional Chilean accompaniments such as pebre (a spicy salsa), bread, and Chilean wine or beer.

Enjoy this delicious and traditional Chilean dish with friends and family for a memorable dining experience!

Leche Asada

Ingredients:

- 4 cups milk
- 4 eggs
- 1 cup granulated sugar
- 1 teaspoon vanilla extract
- Ground cinnamon, for garnish (optional)

Instructions:

1. Preheat your oven to 350°F (175°C). Lightly grease a baking dish with butter or cooking spray.
2. In a saucepan, heat the milk over medium heat until it just begins to simmer. Remove from heat and let it cool slightly.
3. In a mixing bowl, whisk together the eggs, sugar, and vanilla extract until well combined.
4. Slowly pour the warm milk into the egg mixture, whisking constantly, until smooth and well incorporated.
5. Strain the mixture through a fine-mesh sieve into the prepared baking dish to remove any lumps.
6. Place the baking dish in a larger roasting pan or baking dish. Carefully pour hot water into the larger pan, being careful not to splash any water into the Leche Asada mixture. The water should come about halfway up the sides of the baking dish.
7. Place the pan in the preheated oven and bake for about 45-55 minutes, or until the Leche Asada is set and golden on top. It should jiggle slightly in the center when gently shaken.
8. Remove the pan from the oven and let the Leche Asada cool to room temperature.
9. Once cooled, cover the baking dish with plastic wrap and refrigerate the Leche Asada for at least 2 hours, or until thoroughly chilled and set.
10. To serve, cut the Leche Asada into squares or slices and garnish with ground cinnamon, if desired.
11. Enjoy this creamy and comforting Chilean dessert as a sweet treat after a meal or as a snack any time of day!

Leche Asada can be stored in the refrigerator for up to 3 days. Just be sure to cover it tightly to prevent it from drying out. Enjoy!

Sopa de Mariscos

Ingredients:

- 1 lb assorted seafood (fish fillets, shrimp, clams, mussels, etc.), cleaned and deveined
- 1 onion, chopped
- 2 cloves garlic, minced
- 2 carrots, diced
- 2 stalks celery, diced
- 1 red bell pepper, diced
- 1 can (14 oz) diced tomatoes
- 4 cups fish or seafood broth
- 1 cup white wine (optional)
- 1 teaspoon paprika
- 1/2 teaspoon dried thyme
- Salt and pepper to taste
- Fresh parsley or cilantro, chopped, for garnish
- Lemon wedges, for serving
- Crusty bread, for serving

Instructions:

1. In a large pot or Dutch oven, heat a drizzle of olive oil over medium heat. Add the chopped onion and garlic and sauté until softened and fragrant, about 5 minutes.
2. Add the diced carrots, celery, and red bell pepper to the pot. Cook for another 5 minutes, stirring occasionally, until the vegetables start to soften.
3. Pour in the diced tomatoes (with their juices) and cook for a few minutes to let the flavors meld together.
4. Add the fish or seafood broth to the pot, along with the white wine (if using). Bring the mixture to a simmer.
5. Season the broth with paprika, dried thyme, salt, and pepper to taste. Adjust the seasoning as needed.
6. Carefully add the assorted seafood to the pot, making sure it is submerged in the broth. Cover the pot and simmer gently for about 10-15 minutes, or until the seafood is cooked through and opaque.
7. Once the seafood is cooked, remove the pot from the heat. Taste the broth and adjust the seasoning if necessary.

8. Ladle the Sopa de Mariscos into serving bowls and garnish with chopped fresh parsley or cilantro.
9. Serve the soup hot, accompanied by lemon wedges for squeezing over the seafood, and crusty bread for dipping.
10. Enjoy this delicious and comforting Sopa de Mariscos as a satisfying meal on its own or as a starter for a larger seafood feast!

Feel free to customize the soup with your favorite seafood and vegetables, and adjust the seasonings to suit your taste preferences. Buon appetito!

Tomatican

Ingredients:

- 1 lb ground beef
- 2 tablespoons vegetable oil
- 1 onion, chopped
- 2 cloves garlic, minced
- 4 large tomatoes, diced
- 4 potatoes, peeled and diced
- 1 teaspoon paprika
- 1/2 teaspoon ground cumin
- Salt and pepper to taste
- Fresh parsley or cilantro, chopped, for garnish

Instructions:

1. Heat the vegetable oil in a large skillet or pot over medium heat. Add the chopped onion and minced garlic and sauté until softened and fragrant, about 5 minutes.
2. Add the ground beef to the skillet and cook, breaking it apart with a spoon, until browned and cooked through, about 5-7 minutes.
3. Once the beef is cooked, add the diced tomatoes to the skillet, along with the paprika, ground cumin, salt, and pepper. Stir to combine.
4. Add the diced potatoes to the skillet and stir to incorporate them into the beef and tomato mixture.
5. Cover the skillet and let the Tomatican simmer gently over medium-low heat for about 20-25 minutes, or until the potatoes are tender and cooked through.
6. Once the potatoes are cooked, taste the Tomatican and adjust the seasoning as needed with additional salt and pepper.
7. Remove the skillet from the heat and sprinkle the chopped fresh parsley or cilantro over the top for garnish.
8. Serve the Tomatican hot, straight from the skillet, as a delicious and comforting meal on its own.
9. Enjoy the hearty flavors of this traditional Chilean dish, and savor each bite of tender beef, tomatoes, and potatoes!

Feel free to customize the Tomatican with additional vegetables or spices, according to your taste preferences. You can also serve it with rice or crusty bread on the side for a complete meal. Buon appetito!

Sopa de Porotos

Ingredients:

- 2 cups dried beans (white beans, pinto beans, or kidney beans), soaked overnight
- 1 onion, chopped
- 2 cloves garlic, minced
- 2 carrots, diced
- 2 celery stalks, diced
- 1 tomato, diced
- 1 teaspoon ground cumin
- 1 teaspoon paprika
- 1 bay leaf
- 6 cups vegetable or chicken broth
- Salt and pepper to taste
- 2 tablespoons olive oil
- Fresh cilantro or parsley for garnish (optional)

Instructions:

1. Drain and rinse the soaked beans under cold water. Set aside.
2. In a large pot, heat olive oil over medium heat. Add chopped onion and cook until translucent, about 3-4 minutes.
3. Add minced garlic, diced carrots, diced celery, and diced tomato to the pot. Cook for another 5 minutes, stirring occasionally.
4. Stir in the soaked beans, ground cumin, paprika, bay leaf, and broth. Bring the mixture to a boil, then reduce the heat to low. Cover and simmer for about 1 to 1.5 hours, or until the beans are tender.
5. Once the beans are tender, season the soup with salt and pepper to taste. Adjust seasoning as needed.
6. If desired, remove the bay leaf from the soup before serving.
7. Ladle the Sopa de Porotos into bowls and garnish with fresh cilantro or parsley, if using.
8. Serve hot and enjoy!

This hearty bean soup is perfect for chilly days and makes a satisfying meal when served with crusty bread or rice. Enjoy!

Pan Amasado

Ingredients:

- 4 cups all-purpose flour
- 2 teaspoons active dry yeast
- 1 teaspoon salt
- 2 tablespoons granulated sugar
- 2 tablespoons vegetable oil
- 1 1/4 cups warm water

Instructions:

1. In a large mixing bowl, combine the warm water and granulated sugar. Stir until the sugar is dissolved.
2. Sprinkle the active dry yeast over the water and let it sit for about 5-10 minutes, or until it becomes frothy.
3. Once the yeast is activated, add the vegetable oil to the yeast mixture and stir to combine.
4. In another large mixing bowl, sift together the all-purpose flour and salt.
5. Gradually add the flour mixture to the yeast mixture, stirring with a wooden spoon until a dough forms.
6. Once the dough comes together, transfer it to a floured surface and knead it for about 8-10 minutes, or until it becomes smooth and elastic.
7. Shape the dough into a ball and place it back into the mixing bowl. Cover the bowl with a clean kitchen towel or plastic wrap and let the dough rise in a warm, draft-free place for about 1-1.5 hours, or until it has doubled in size.
8. After the dough has risen, punch it down to release any air bubbles.
9. Preheat the oven to 375°F (190°C). Line a baking sheet with parchment paper.
10. Divide the dough into small portions, about the size of a golf ball, and shape each portion into a small round bun.
11. Place the buns onto the prepared baking sheet, leaving some space between each bun.
12. Cover the buns with a clean kitchen towel and let them rise for another 30-45 minutes, or until they have doubled in size.
13. Once the buns have risen, bake them in the preheated oven for 15-20 minutes, or until they are golden brown on top and sound hollow when tapped on the bottom.
14. Remove the buns from the oven and let them cool on a wire rack before serving.

Enjoy your homemade Pan Amasado warm with butter or as an accompaniment to your favorite Chilean dishes!

Milcaos

Ingredients:

- 4 large potatoes (preferably starchy varieties like russet or Yukon Gold)
- 1/2 cup cooked mashed potatoes (optional, for binding)
- 1/2 cup all-purpose flour (optional, for binding)
- Salt, to taste
- Vegetable oil, for frying

Instructions:

1. Peel the potatoes and grate them using a box grater or a food processor with a grating attachment.
2. Place the grated potatoes in a clean kitchen towel and squeeze out as much liquid as possible.
3. Transfer the squeezed potatoes to a large mixing bowl. If using, add the cooked mashed potatoes and flour to the bowl for binding. Season with salt to taste.
4. Mix the ingredients together until well combined. The mixture should be moist but not overly wet.
5. Heat a skillet or griddle over medium heat and add enough vegetable oil to coat the bottom.
6. Take a portion of the potato mixture and shape it into a round pancake, about 1/2 inch thick. You can use your hands or a spoon to shape the pancakes.
7. Carefully place the pancake onto the hot skillet or griddle and flatten it slightly with a spatula.
8. Cook the milcao for about 5-7 minutes on each side, or until golden brown and crispy.
9. Once cooked, transfer the milcao to a plate lined with paper towels to drain any excess oil.
10. Repeat the process with the remaining potato mixture, adding more oil to the skillet or griddle as needed.
11. Serve the milcaos warm as a side dish or snack.

Enjoy your homemade milcaos with a dollop of sour cream or your favorite dipping sauce!

Arrollado Huaso

Ingredients:

- 2 pounds pork belly, skin-on
- 2 tablespoons vegetable oil
- 1 onion, finely chopped
- 2 cloves garlic, minced
- 1 teaspoon ground cumin
- 1 teaspoon paprika
- 1 teaspoon dried oregano
- Salt and pepper, to taste
- 1/2 cup white wine (optional)
- Kitchen twine

Instructions:

1. Preheat your oven to 350°F (175°C).
2. In a large skillet, heat the vegetable oil over medium heat. Add the chopped onion and minced garlic, and sauté until softened and fragrant.
3. Season the pork belly generously with salt, pepper, ground cumin, paprika, and dried oregano.
4. Lay the pork belly flat on a clean surface, skin-side down. Spread the sautéed onion and garlic mixture evenly over the meat.
5. Starting from one end, tightly roll up the pork belly into a log shape. Tie the roll securely with kitchen twine at regular intervals to hold its shape.
6. Place the rolled pork belly in a large pot and add enough water to cover it. If using, pour in the white wine.
7. Bring the water to a boil over high heat, then reduce the heat to low and simmer the pork roll, covered, for about 1.5 to 2 hours, or until the meat is tender.
8. Once cooked, remove the pork roll from the pot and let it cool slightly.
9. Remove the kitchen twine from the pork roll and slice it into thick rounds.
10. Optionally, you can sear the slices in a hot skillet to crisp up the edges before serving.
11. Serve the Arrollado Huaso slices warm or at room temperature, accompanied by traditional Chilean pebre (a type of salsa) or a simple salad.

Enjoy the flavors of this classic Chilean dish, perfect for gatherings or special occasions!

Calapurca

Ingredients:

- 1 pound beef or pork, cubed
- 1 tablespoon vegetable oil
- 1 onion, chopped
- 2 cloves garlic, minced
- 2 tomatoes, chopped
- 2 carrots, diced
- 2 potatoes, peeled and diced
- 1 cup green peas
- 1 cup corn kernels
- 6 cups beef or vegetable broth
- 1 teaspoon ground cumin
- 1 teaspoon dried oregano
- Salt and pepper, to taste
- Fresh cilantro or parsley, chopped, for garnish (optional)

Instructions:

1. In a large pot, heat the vegetable oil over medium heat. Add the chopped onion and minced garlic, and sauté until softened and fragrant.
2. Add the cubed meat to the pot and cook until browned on all sides.
3. Stir in the chopped tomatoes, diced carrots, diced potatoes, green peas, and corn kernels. Cook for a few minutes, stirring occasionally.
4. Pour in the beef or vegetable broth and bring the soup to a boil.
5. Reduce the heat to low and simmer the soup, covered, for about 30-40 minutes, or until the meat and vegetables are tender.
6. Season the soup with ground cumin, dried oregano, salt, and pepper, adjusting to taste.
7. Serve the Calapurca hot, garnished with fresh cilantro or parsley if desired.

Enjoy this hearty and comforting Ecuadorian soup, perfect for chilly days!

Alfajores

Ingredients:

- 1 cup cornstarch
- 3/4 cup all-purpose flour
- 1 teaspoon baking powder
- 1/2 teaspoon baking soda
- 1/4 teaspoon salt
- 1/2 cup unsalted butter, softened
- 1/3 cup granulated sugar
- 2 large egg yolks
- 1 teaspoon vanilla extract
- Dulce de leche, for filling
- Powdered sugar, for dusting (optional)

Instructions:

1. In a mixing bowl, sift together the cornstarch, all-purpose flour, baking powder, baking soda, and salt. Set aside.
2. In a separate bowl, cream together the softened butter and granulated sugar until light and fluffy.
3. Add the egg yolks and vanilla extract to the butter-sugar mixture, and beat until well combined.
4. Gradually add the dry ingredients to the wet ingredients, mixing until a smooth dough forms.
5. Shape the dough into a ball, wrap it in plastic wrap, and refrigerate for at least 30 minutes to firm up.
6. Preheat your oven to 350°F (175°C). Line a baking sheet with parchment paper.
7. Roll out the chilled dough on a lightly floured surface to about 1/4 inch thickness. Use a round cookie cutter to cut out circles of dough.
8. Place the dough circles onto the prepared baking sheet, spacing them a few inches apart.
9. Bake the cookies in the preheated oven for about 10-12 minutes, or until they are lightly golden around the edges.
10. Remove the cookies from the oven and let them cool completely on a wire rack.
11. Once the cookies are cool, spread a layer of dulce de leche onto the bottom side of half of the cookies.
12. Top each dulce de leche-covered cookie with another cookie to form sandwiches.

13. Optional: Dust the tops of the alfajores with powdered sugar for a decorative touch.
14. Store the alfajores in an airtight container at room temperature for up to several days.

Enjoy these delightful Alfajores with a cup of coffee or tea for a sweet and indulgent treat!

Estofado de Pollo

Ingredients:

- 1 whole chicken, cut into pieces (or use bone-in chicken thighs and drumsticks)
- 2 tablespoons olive oil
- 1 onion, chopped
- 2 cloves garlic, minced
- 2 carrots, peeled and diced
- 2 potatoes, peeled and diced
- 1 red bell pepper, diced
- 1 green bell pepper, diced
- 1 cup frozen peas
- 1 can (14 oz) diced tomatoes
- 2 cups chicken broth
- 1 teaspoon paprika
- 1 teaspoon ground cumin
- 1/2 teaspoon dried oregano
- Salt and pepper, to taste
- Fresh parsley, chopped, for garnish (optional)

Instructions:

1. Season the chicken pieces with salt, pepper, paprika, and ground cumin.
2. In a large pot or Dutch oven, heat the olive oil over medium heat. Add the seasoned chicken pieces and brown them on all sides. Remove the chicken from the pot and set aside.
3. In the same pot, add the chopped onion and minced garlic. Sauté until softened and fragrant.
4. Add the diced carrots, potatoes, red bell pepper, and green bell pepper to the pot. Cook for a few minutes until the vegetables begin to soften.
5. Return the browned chicken pieces to the pot.
6. Pour in the diced tomatoes (with their juices) and chicken broth. Stir to combine.
7. Add the dried oregano and adjust the seasoning with salt and pepper to taste.
8. Bring the stew to a simmer, then reduce the heat to low. Cover and cook for about 30-40 minutes, or until the chicken is cooked through and the vegetables are tender.
9. Stir in the frozen peas and cook for an additional 5 minutes.
10. Taste and adjust the seasoning if needed.

11. Serve the Estofado de Pollo hot, garnished with chopped fresh parsley if desired.

Enjoy this hearty and flavorful Spanish chicken stew with crusty bread or rice for a satisfying meal!

Pastel de Papas

Ingredients:

- 2 pounds potatoes, peeled and cut into chunks
- Salt, to taste
- 2 tablespoons butter
- 1/2 cup milk (or more, as needed)
- 2 tablespoons olive oil
- 1 onion, chopped
- 2 cloves garlic, minced
- 1 pound ground beef or ground lamb
- 1 teaspoon paprika
- 1/2 teaspoon ground cumin
- Salt and pepper, to taste
- 1 cup diced carrots (optional)
- 1 cup frozen peas (optional)
- 1 cup corn kernels (optional)
- 1/2 cup beef or vegetable broth (if needed)

Instructions:

1. Place the peeled and chopped potatoes in a large pot of salted water. Bring to a boil and cook until the potatoes are fork-tender, about 15-20 minutes.
2. Drain the potatoes and return them to the pot. Add the butter and milk, then mash the potatoes until smooth and creamy. Season with salt to taste. Set aside.
3. Preheat your oven to 375°F (190°C).
4. In a large skillet, heat the olive oil over medium heat. Add the chopped onion and minced garlic, and sauté until softened and fragrant.
5. Add the ground beef or lamb to the skillet and cook until browned, breaking it up with a spoon as it cooks.
6. Stir in the paprika, ground cumin, salt, and pepper. If using, add the diced carrots, frozen peas, and corn kernels. Cook for a few minutes until the vegetables are tender.
7. If the mixture seems dry, you can add some beef or vegetable broth to moisten it.
8. Transfer the meat and vegetable mixture to a baking dish, spreading it out evenly.
9. Spread the mashed potatoes over the top of the meat mixture, smoothing it out with a spatula.

10. Place the baking dish in the preheated oven and bake for about 25-30 minutes, or until the top is golden brown and the filling is bubbling.
11. Remove from the oven and let it cool for a few minutes before serving.

Enjoy this comforting and hearty Argentine Potato Pie as a satisfying meal for lunch or dinner!

Kuchen

Ingredients:

- 2 cups all-purpose flour
- 1/2 cup granulated sugar
- 1/2 cup unsalted butter, softened
- 1 large egg
- 1 teaspoon baking powder
- Pinch of salt
- 1/2 cup milk
- 1 teaspoon vanilla extract
- Sliced fruit (such as apples, peaches, or plums)
- 2 tablespoons granulated sugar (for fruit topping)
- 1 teaspoon ground cinnamon (optional, for fruit topping)
- Powdered sugar, for dusting (optional)

Instructions:

1. Preheat your oven to 350°F (175°C). Grease and flour a 9-inch round cake pan or tart pan.
2. In a large mixing bowl, cream together the softened butter and granulated sugar until light and fluffy.
3. Add the egg and vanilla extract to the butter-sugar mixture, and beat until well combined.
4. In a separate bowl, sift together the all-purpose flour, baking powder, and salt.
5. Gradually add the dry ingredients to the wet ingredients, alternating with the milk, and mix until a smooth batter forms.
6. Pour the batter into the prepared cake or tart pan, spreading it out evenly with a spatula.
7. Arrange the sliced fruit on top of the batter in a decorative pattern. Sprinkle the fruit with granulated sugar and ground cinnamon, if desired.
8. Bake the Kuchen in the preheated oven for 30-40 minutes, or until the cake is golden brown and a toothpick inserted into the center comes out clean.
9. Remove the Kuchen from the oven and let it cool in the pan for a few minutes before transferring it to a wire rack to cool completely.
10. Once cooled, dust the Kuchen with powdered sugar, if desired.
11. Slice and serve the Kuchen as a delicious dessert or snack.

Enjoy this classic German cake with a cup of coffee or tea for a delightful treat!

Pastel de Jaiba

Ingredients:

- 1 pound crab meat, cooked and shredded
- 1 tablespoon olive oil
- 1 onion, finely chopped
- 2 cloves garlic, minced
- 1 red bell pepper, diced
- 1 green bell pepper, diced
- 1 cup frozen corn kernels
- 1 cup frozen peas
- 1 cup diced tomatoes
- 1 teaspoon paprika
- 1/2 teaspoon ground cumin
- Salt and pepper, to taste
- 1/2 cup milk
- 2 tablespoons all-purpose flour
- 2 eggs, beaten
- 1/2 cup grated cheese (such as Parmesan or Cheddar)
- Bread crumbs, for topping
- Fresh parsley, chopped, for garnish (optional)

Instructions:

1. Preheat your oven to 350°F (175°C). Grease a baking dish or pie dish with butter or oil.
2. In a large skillet, heat the olive oil over medium heat. Add the chopped onion and minced garlic, and sauté until softened and fragrant.
3. Add the diced red and green bell peppers to the skillet, and cook for a few minutes until they begin to soften.
4. Stir in the frozen corn kernels, frozen peas, diced tomatoes, paprika, ground cumin, salt, and pepper. Cook for another 5 minutes, stirring occasionally.
5. In a small bowl, whisk together the milk and all-purpose flour until smooth. Pour this mixture into the skillet and stir until well combined. Cook for an additional 2-3 minutes, until the mixture thickens slightly.
6. Remove the skillet from the heat and let the mixture cool slightly.
7. In a separate bowl, combine the shredded crab meat, beaten eggs, and grated cheese. Mix until evenly distributed.

8. Fold the crab mixture into the vegetable mixture in the skillet until well combined.
9. Transfer the mixture to the prepared baking dish or pie dish, spreading it out evenly.
10. Sprinkle bread crumbs over the top of the mixture to form a crust.
11. Bake the Pastel de Jaiba in the preheated oven for 25-30 minutes, or until the top is golden brown and the filling is set.
12. Remove from the oven and let it cool for a few minutes before serving.
13. Garnish with chopped fresh parsley, if desired, before serving.

Enjoy this flavorful and hearty Chilean Crab Pie as a main dish for lunch or dinner!

Sopa de Zapallo

Ingredients:

- 1 medium zapallo (squash or pumpkin), peeled, seeded, and diced
- 1 onion, chopped
- 2 cloves garlic, minced
- 2 carrots, peeled and diced
- 2 potatoes, peeled and diced
- 6 cups vegetable or chicken broth
- 1 teaspoon ground cumin
- 1 teaspoon paprika
- 1 bay leaf
- Salt and pepper, to taste
- 2 tablespoons olive oil
- Fresh cilantro or parsley, chopped, for garnish (optional)

Instructions:

1. In a large pot, heat olive oil over medium heat. Add chopped onion and cook until translucent, about 3-4 minutes.
2. Add minced garlic to the pot and cook for another minute until fragrant.
3. Add diced zapallo, carrots, and potatoes to the pot. Cook for a few minutes, stirring occasionally.
4. Pour in the vegetable or chicken broth, enough to cover the vegetables. Add the ground cumin, paprika, and bay leaf to the pot. Season with salt and pepper to taste.
5. Bring the soup to a boil, then reduce the heat to low. Cover and simmer for about 20-25 minutes, or until the vegetables are tender.
6. Once the vegetables are cooked, remove the bay leaf from the soup.
7. Use an immersion blender or transfer the soup in batches to a blender to puree until smooth.
8. If the soup is too thick, you can add more broth or water to reach your desired consistency.
9. Taste and adjust the seasoning if needed.
10. Ladle the Sopa de Zapallo into bowls and garnish with fresh cilantro or parsley, if using.
11. Serve hot and enjoy!

This creamy and comforting Chilean Pumpkin Soup is perfect for colder days and makes a delicious starter or light meal.

Curanto en Olla

Ingredients:

- 1 pound mussels, cleaned and debearded
- 1 pound clams, cleaned
- 1 pound shrimp, peeled and deveined
- 1 pound fish fillets (such as salmon or cod), cut into chunks
- 1 pound chicken thighs, bone-in
- 1 pound pork sausages (such as chorizo or longaniza), sliced
- 1 pound pork ribs, cut into pieces
- 1 pound beef ribs, cut into pieces
- 1 pound pork belly or bacon, sliced
- 2 pounds potatoes, peeled and halved
- 2 pounds sweet potatoes or yams, peeled and halved
- 2 pounds ripe tomatoes, halved
- 2 large onions, sliced
- 2 cloves garlic, minced
- 2 cups white wine
- 2 cups chicken or vegetable broth
- 1/4 cup olive oil
- Salt and pepper, to taste
- Fresh cilantro or parsley, chopped, for garnish (optional)

Instructions:

1. In a large pot, heat the olive oil over medium heat. Add the minced garlic and sliced onions, and sauté until softened and fragrant.
2. Layer the ingredients in the pot starting with the potatoes and sweet potatoes at the bottom, followed by the tomatoes, chicken thighs, pork ribs, beef ribs, pork belly or bacon, pork sausages, mussels, clams, shrimp, and fish fillets.
3. Season each layer with salt and pepper as desired.
4. Pour the white wine and chicken or vegetable broth over the layered ingredients.
5. Cover the pot with a tight-fitting lid and bring the liquid to a boil over high heat.
6. Once boiling, reduce the heat to low and simmer the Curanto en Olla for about 1.5 to 2 hours, or until all the ingredients are tender and cooked through.
7. Carefully remove the lid and check the seasoning. Adjust with salt and pepper if needed.

8. Serve the Curanto en Olla hot, garnished with chopped fresh cilantro or parsley if desired.

This rich and flavorful Chilean stew is perfect for sharing with friends and family, especially on special occasions or gatherings. Enjoy the delicious combination of seafood, meat, and vegetables cooked together in one pot!

Pernil de Cerdo

Ingredients:

- 1 bone-in pork leg or shoulder (about 5-7 pounds)
- 8 cloves garlic, minced
- 1/4 cup orange juice
- 1/4 cup lime juice
- 1/4 cup olive oil
- 2 tablespoons white vinegar
- 2 teaspoons dried oregano
- 2 teaspoons ground cumin
- 2 teaspoons paprika
- 1 teaspoon ground black pepper
- 2 teaspoons salt
- 1 onion, thinly sliced
- 2 bay leaves
- 1 cup chicken or vegetable broth

Instructions:

1. Using a sharp knife, make several deep cuts all over the surface of the pork leg or shoulder.
2. In a bowl, combine the minced garlic, orange juice, lime juice, olive oil, white vinegar, dried oregano, ground cumin, paprika, black pepper, and salt to make the marinade.
3. Place the pork in a large resealable plastic bag or a shallow dish, and pour the marinade over the pork, making sure it's well coated. Seal the bag or cover the dish with plastic wrap, and refrigerate for at least 4 hours, or preferably overnight, to marinate.
4. Preheat your oven to 325°F (160°C).
5. Remove the marinated pork from the refrigerator and let it come to room temperature for about 30 minutes.
6. Transfer the pork to a roasting pan or baking dish. Arrange the sliced onion and bay leaves around the pork.
7. Pour the chicken or vegetable broth into the bottom of the roasting pan.
8. Cover the pork loosely with aluminum foil and roast in the preheated oven for about 3 to 4 hours, or until the internal temperature of the pork reaches 165°F (75°C) and the meat is tender and falling off the bone.

9. Occasionally baste the pork with the pan juices while it roasts.
10. Once cooked, remove the foil and increase the oven temperature to 425°F (220°C). Return the pork to the oven and roast for an additional 15-20 minutes, or until the skin is crispy and golden brown.
11. Remove the pork from the oven and let it rest for about 15 minutes before slicing.
12. Slice the Pernil de Cerdo and serve hot, accompanied by your favorite side dishes.

Enjoy this flavorful and succulent Latin American roast pork with family and friends!

Sopa de Lentejas

Ingredients:

- 1 cup dried lentils, rinsed and drained
- 6 cups vegetable or chicken broth
- 1 onion, chopped
- 2 carrots, diced
- 2 celery stalks, diced
- 2 cloves garlic, minced
- 1 potato, diced
- 1 can (14 oz) diced tomatoes
- 1 teaspoon ground cumin
- 1 teaspoon paprika
- 1 bay leaf
- Salt and pepper, to taste
- 2 tablespoons olive oil
- Fresh cilantro or parsley, chopped, for garnish (optional)
- Lemon wedges, for serving (optional)

Instructions:

1. In a large pot, heat olive oil over medium heat. Add chopped onion, diced carrots, diced celery, and minced garlic. Sauté until the vegetables are softened, about 5-7 minutes.
2. Add the rinsed lentils, diced potato, diced tomatoes (with their juices), ground cumin, paprika, bay leaf, salt, and pepper to the pot. Stir to combine.
3. Pour in the vegetable or chicken broth and bring the soup to a boil.
4. Once boiling, reduce the heat to low and simmer the soup, covered, for about 25-30 minutes, or until the lentils and vegetables are tender.
5. If the soup becomes too thick during cooking, you can add more broth or water to reach your desired consistency.
6. Taste and adjust the seasoning if needed.
7. Remove the bay leaf from the soup before serving.
8. Ladle the Sopa de Lentejas into bowls and garnish with chopped fresh cilantro or parsley, if desired.
9. Serve hot with lemon wedges on the side for squeezing over the soup, if desired.

This Sopa de Lentejas is not only delicious and comforting but also packed with protein and fiber from the lentils and vegetables. Enjoy it as a satisfying meal on its own or paired with crusty bread for a complete and nutritious dish!

Humitas en Olla

Ingredients:

- 6 ears of fresh corn, husks removed and kernels grated (or 3 cups of canned corn kernels, drained)
- 1 onion, finely chopped
- 2 tablespoons vegetable oil
- 1/2 cup milk
- 1/4 cup butter, melted
- 1/2 cup cornmeal
- 1/4 cup all-purpose flour
- 1 teaspoon baking powder
- Salt, to taste
- 1 cup grated cheese (such as mozzarella or Monterey Jack)
- Corn husks or banana leaves, soaked in water for 30 minutes

Instructions:

1. In a large skillet, heat the vegetable oil over medium heat. Add the chopped onion and cook until softened and translucent, about 5 minutes. Remove from heat and let it cool.
2. In a large mixing bowl, combine the grated corn, cooked onion, milk, melted butter, cornmeal, all-purpose flour, baking powder, and salt. Mix well to form a thick batter.
3. Take a corn husk or banana leaf and place a spoonful of the corn batter onto the center of the husk or leaf. Flatten the batter slightly and sprinkle some grated cheese on top.
4. Fold the sides of the husk or leaf over the batter to enclose it completely, forming a rectangular or square packet. Tie the packet securely with kitchen twine.
5. Repeat the process with the remaining batter and corn husks or banana leaves until all the batter is used.
6. In a large pot, bring water to a boil. Place a steamer basket or colander in the pot, making sure the water doesn't touch the bottom of the basket.
7. Arrange the wrapped Humitas en Olla in the steamer basket or colander, making sure they are not overcrowded.
8. Cover the pot with a lid and steam the Humitas en Olla over medium heat for about 45-60 minutes, or until the corn cakes are firm and cooked through.

9. Remove the Humitas en Olla from the steamer and let them cool slightly before serving.
10. Unwrap the corn cakes from the husks or leaves before serving.

Humitas en Olla are typically served warm as a snack or side dish. Enjoy the delicious flavors of these steamed corn cakes, filled with cheesy goodness!

Chapalele

Ingredients:

- 4 large potatoes, peeled and grated
- 1 cup all-purpose flour
- 1/2 teaspoon salt
- Water, as needed
- 1 cup sugar
- 1 cinnamon stick
- 1 lemon peel (optional)
- 1 cup water

Instructions:

1. In a large mixing bowl, combine the grated potatoes, all-purpose flour, and salt. Mix well to form a dough.
2. If the dough is too dry, add a little water, a tablespoon at a time, until it comes together.
3. Divide the dough into small portions and shape each portion into a round dumpling.
4. In a large pot, bring water to a boil. Carefully add the dumplings to the boiling water, making sure not to overcrowd the pot.
5. Boil the dumplings for about 15-20 minutes, or until they float to the surface and are cooked through.
6. While the dumplings are cooking, prepare the syrup. In a separate pot, combine the sugar, cinnamon stick, lemon peel (if using), and water. Bring to a boil, then reduce the heat and simmer for about 10 minutes to thicken slightly.
7. Once the dumplings are cooked, remove them from the water using a slotted spoon and transfer them to serving plates.
8. Pour the syrup over the dumplings and serve warm.

Chapalele is often enjoyed as a dessert or sweet treat in Chile, especially during the colder months. The combination of soft potato dumplings and sweet syrup makes for a comforting and satisfying dish.

Chilenitos

Ingredients:

For the cookies:

- 2 cups all-purpose flour
- 1/2 cup powdered sugar
- 1/2 teaspoon baking powder
- 1/4 teaspoon salt
- 1/2 cup unsalted butter, softened
- 1 large egg
- 1 teaspoon vanilla extract

For the filling:

- Dulce de leche (store-bought or homemade)

For dusting:

- Powdered sugar

Instructions:

1. Preheat your oven to 350°F (175°C). Line a baking sheet with parchment paper.
2. In a mixing bowl, sift together the all-purpose flour, powdered sugar, baking powder, and salt.
3. Add the softened butter to the dry ingredients, and use your hands or a pastry cutter to mix until the mixture resembles coarse crumbs.
4. In a small bowl, whisk together the egg and vanilla extract. Pour the egg mixture into the dry ingredients and mix until a dough forms.
5. Transfer the dough to a lightly floured surface and knead gently until smooth.
6. Roll out the dough to about 1/4 inch thickness. Use a round cookie cutter to cut out cookies. You'll need an even number of cookies.
7. Place the cookies onto the prepared baking sheet, spacing them a few inches apart.

8. Bake the cookies in the preheated oven for about 10-12 minutes, or until they are just starting to turn golden around the edges.
9. Remove the cookies from the oven and let them cool completely on a wire rack.
10. Once the cookies are cool, spread a layer of dulce de leche onto the bottom side of half of the cookies.
11. Top each dulce de leche-covered cookie with another cookie to form sandwiches.
12. Dust the tops of the Chilenitos with powdered sugar for a decorative touch.

Enjoy these delicious Chilenitos as a sweet treat with a cup of coffee or tea! They're perfect for special occasions or whenever you're craving something indulgent.

Cola de Mono

Ingredients:

- 2 cups whole milk
- 1/2 cup granulated sugar
- 1/2 cup water
- 1 cinnamon stick
- 6 cloves
- 1 tablespoon instant coffee granules
- 1 teaspoon vanilla extract
- 1 cup pisco or white rum
- Ice cubes, for serving
- Ground cinnamon, for garnish (optional)

Instructions:

1. In a saucepan, combine the whole milk, granulated sugar, water, cinnamon stick, and cloves. Heat the mixture over medium heat, stirring occasionally, until it starts to simmer and the sugar has dissolved.
2. Reduce the heat to low and let the mixture simmer gently for about 5 minutes to infuse the flavors of the spices.
3. Remove the saucepan from the heat and stir in the instant coffee granules until dissolved.
4. Let the mixture cool to room temperature, then strain it through a fine mesh sieve to remove the cinnamon stick and cloves.
5. Stir in the vanilla extract and pisco or white rum until well combined.
6. Transfer the Cola de Mono to a pitcher or bottle and refrigerate until chilled.
7. To serve, fill glasses with ice cubes and pour the chilled Cola de Mono over the ice.
8. Optionally, garnish each glass with a sprinkle of ground cinnamon before serving.

Enjoy this festive and delicious Cola de Mono with family and friends during the holiday season! It's perfect for sipping and celebrating. Remember to enjoy responsibly.

Chupe de Locos

Ingredients:

- 1 pound locos (abalone), cleaned and sliced
- 1 onion, finely chopped
- 2 cloves garlic, minced
- 2 tablespoons vegetable oil
- 2 tomatoes, diced
- 1 bell pepper, diced
- 1 cup frozen corn kernels
- 1 cup frozen peas
- 4 cups fish or seafood broth
- 1 cup heavy cream
- 1/2 teaspoon ground cumin
- 1/2 teaspoon paprika
- Salt and pepper, to taste
- Fresh cilantro or parsley, chopped, for garnish (optional)
- Lemon wedges, for serving (optional)

Instructions:

1. In a large pot, heat the vegetable oil over medium heat. Add the chopped onion and minced garlic, and sauté until softened and fragrant.
2. Add the sliced locos to the pot and cook for a few minutes until they start to brown.
3. Stir in the diced tomatoes, bell pepper, frozen corn kernels, and frozen peas. Cook for another 5 minutes, stirring occasionally.
4. Pour in the fish or seafood broth and bring the mixture to a simmer.
5. Add the ground cumin, paprika, salt, and pepper to the pot. Stir to combine.
6. Let the stew simmer for about 15-20 minutes, allowing the flavors to meld together and the locos to become tender.
7. Once the locos are cooked through and the vegetables are tender, stir in the heavy cream. Cook for an additional 5 minutes, stirring occasionally.
8. Taste and adjust the seasoning if needed.
9. Serve the Chupe de Locos hot, garnished with chopped fresh cilantro or parsley if desired, and accompanied by lemon wedges for squeezing over the stew.

Enjoy this comforting and flavorful Chilean seafood stew with crusty bread or rice for a satisfying meal! It's perfect for sharing with family and friends on special occasions or gatherings.

Chirimoya Sour

Ingredients:

- 2 ounces pisco
- 1 ounce chirimoya pulp (strained)
- 1/2 ounce fresh lime juice
- 1/2 ounce simple syrup
- 1/2 egg white
- Ice cubes
- Angostura bitters, for garnish
- Chirimoya slice or lime wheel, for garnish

Instructions:

1. In a cocktail shaker, combine the pisco, chirimoya pulp, fresh lime juice, simple syrup, and egg white.
2. Fill the shaker with ice cubes and shake vigorously for about 15-20 seconds to chill the mixture and froth the egg white.
3. Strain the cocktail into a chilled glass filled with ice.
4. Garnish the Chirimoya Sour with a few dashes of Angostura bitters on top.
5. Optionally, garnish with a slice of chirimoya or a lime wheel on the rim of the glass.
6. Serve immediately and enjoy!

This Chirimoya Sour is a refreshing and tropical twist on the classic Pisco Sour, perfect for enjoying on a warm day or as a special cocktail for celebrations. Adjust the sweetness to your taste by adding more or less simple syrup. Cheers!

Machas a la Parmesana

Ingredients:

- 12 fresh razor clams (machas), cleaned and opened
- 1/2 cup breadcrumbs
- 1/2 cup grated Parmesan cheese
- 2 cloves garlic, minced
- 1/4 cup fresh parsley, chopped
- 2 tablespoons olive oil
- Salt and pepper, to taste
- Lemon wedges, for serving

Instructions:

1. Preheat your oven to 375°F (190°C).
2. In a small mixing bowl, combine the breadcrumbs, grated Parmesan cheese, minced garlic, chopped parsley, and olive oil. Season with salt and pepper to taste. Mix well to combine.
3. Place the cleaned and opened razor clams on a baking sheet or ovenproof dish.
4. Spoon the breadcrumb mixture evenly over each razor clam, pressing gently to adhere.
5. Bake the Machas a la Parmesana in the preheated oven for about 8-10 minutes, or until the breadcrumbs are golden brown and the clams are heated through.
6. Remove from the oven and let them cool slightly before serving.
7. Serve the Machas a la Parmesana hot, with lemon wedges on the side for squeezing over the clams.

Enjoy these delicious Machas a la Parmesana as a flavorful appetizer or seafood dish, perfect for sharing with family and friends!

Cochayuyo en Ensalada

Ingredients:

- 1 cup dried cochayuyo seaweed
- 1 red bell pepper, diced
- 1 green bell pepper, diced
- 1 onion, finely chopped
- 1 tomato, diced
- 1/4 cup fresh cilantro or parsley, chopped
- 2 tablespoons olive oil
- 2 tablespoons white wine vinegar or lemon juice
- Salt and pepper, to taste

Instructions:

1. Rinse the dried cochayuyo seaweed under cold water to remove any debris or impurities. Soak the seaweed in water for about 30 minutes to rehydrate.
2. After soaking, drain the cochayuyo and cut it into bite-sized pieces.
3. In a large mixing bowl, combine the diced red bell pepper, green bell pepper, onion, tomato, and chopped cilantro or parsley.
4. Add the rehydrated cochayuyo pieces to the bowl with the vegetables.
5. Drizzle the olive oil and white wine vinegar or lemon juice over the salad.
6. Season with salt and pepper to taste.
7. Toss the Cochayuyo Salad until all the ingredients are well combined and evenly coated with the dressing.
8. Let the salad marinate in the refrigerator for at least 30 minutes before serving to allow the flavors to meld together.
9. Serve the Cochayuyo Salad chilled as a refreshing and nutritious appetizer or side dish.

Enjoy this unique and flavorful Cochayuyo Salad as a healthy addition to your meals, showcasing the rich culinary heritage of Chilean cuisine!

Sopa de Zapallo Italiano

Ingredients:

- 4 medium Italian zucchinis, diced
- 1 onion, chopped
- 2 cloves garlic, minced
- 2 tablespoons olive oil
- 4 cups vegetable or chicken broth
- 1 cup milk or cream
- Salt and pepper, to taste
- Fresh basil leaves, chopped, for garnish (optional)
- Grated Parmesan cheese, for garnish (optional)

Instructions:

1. In a large pot, heat the olive oil over medium heat. Add the chopped onion and minced garlic, and sauté until softened and fragrant.
2. Add the diced Italian zucchinis to the pot and cook for a few minutes until they start to soften.
3. Pour in the vegetable or chicken broth and bring the mixture to a simmer. Cook for about 15-20 minutes, or until the zucchinis are tender.
4. Using an immersion blender or transferring the soup to a blender in batches, puree the soup until smooth.
5. Return the pureed soup to the pot and stir in the milk or cream. Heat the soup gently over low heat, stirring occasionally, until warmed through.
6. Season the soup with salt and pepper to taste.
7. Ladle the Sopa de Zapallo Italiano into bowls and garnish with chopped fresh basil leaves and grated Parmesan cheese, if desired.
8. Serve hot and enjoy!

This creamy and flavorful Italian Zucchini Soup is perfect for cooler days and makes a delicious starter or light meal. Serve it with crusty bread for dipping, if desired. Buon appetito!

Sopa de Tortilla

Ingredients:

- 6 corn tortillas, cut into thin strips
- 2 tablespoons vegetable oil
- 1 onion, chopped
- 2 cloves garlic, minced
- 1 jalapeño pepper, seeded and chopped (optional)
- 1 can (14.5 oz) diced tomatoes
- 6 cups chicken or vegetable broth
- 1 teaspoon ground cumin
- 1 teaspoon chili powder
- Salt and pepper, to taste
- 2 cups shredded cooked chicken breast
- 1 avocado, diced
- 1 lime, cut into wedges
- 1/2 cup fresh cilantro leaves, chopped
- 1/2 cup grated cheese (such as Monterey Jack or cheddar)
- Sour cream, for serving (optional)

Instructions:

1. Preheat your oven to 375°F (190°C).
2. Place the tortilla strips on a baking sheet in a single layer. Drizzle with 1 tablespoon of vegetable oil and toss to coat evenly.
3. Bake the tortilla strips in the preheated oven for about 10-12 minutes, or until crispy and golden brown. Remove from the oven and set aside.
4. In a large pot, heat the remaining 1 tablespoon of vegetable oil over medium heat. Add the chopped onion, minced garlic, and chopped jalapeño pepper (if using). Sauté until the vegetables are softened and fragrant.
5. Stir in the diced tomatoes, chicken or vegetable broth, ground cumin, and chili powder. Season with salt and pepper to taste.
6. Bring the soup to a simmer and cook for about 10-15 minutes to allow the flavors to meld together.
7. Add the shredded cooked chicken breast to the soup and simmer for an additional 5 minutes to heat through.
8. Ladle the Sopa de Tortilla into bowls and top with crispy tortilla strips, diced avocado, fresh cilantro leaves, grated cheese, and a squeeze of lime juice.

9. Serve hot, with sour cream on the side if desired.

Enjoy this delicious and comforting Tortilla Soup with all the tasty toppings for a satisfying and flavorful meal!

Charquican de Chuchoca

Ingredients:

- 1 cup chuchoca (coarse cornmeal) or polenta
- 4 cups water or vegetable broth
- 2 tablespoons vegetable oil
- 1 onion, chopped
- 2 cloves garlic, minced
- 2 carrots, diced
- 2 potatoes, diced
- 1 cup pumpkin or squash, diced
- 1 cup frozen corn kernels
- 1 cup cooked beef or chicken, shredded (optional)
- Salt and pepper, to taste
- Fresh cilantro or parsley, chopped, for garnish (optional)

Instructions:

1. In a large pot, bring the water or vegetable broth to a boil.
2. Gradually sprinkle the chuchoca or polenta into the boiling liquid, stirring constantly to prevent lumps from forming.
3. Reduce the heat to low and simmer the cornmeal mixture, stirring occasionally, for about 20-25 minutes or until thickened and cooked through.
4. In a separate skillet, heat the vegetable oil over medium heat. Add the chopped onion and minced garlic, and sauté until softened and fragrant.
5. Add the diced carrots, potatoes, and pumpkin or squash to the skillet. Cook for a few minutes until the vegetables start to soften.
6. Stir in the frozen corn kernels and cooked shredded beef or chicken (if using). Cook for an additional 5-7 minutes, or until the vegetables are tender.
7. Once the vegetables are cooked, transfer the skillet mixture to the pot with the cooked chuchoca or polenta.
8. Mix well to combine all the ingredients. Season with salt and pepper to taste.
9. Let the Charquicán de Chuchoca simmer for a few more minutes to allow the flavors to meld together.
10. Serve the Charquicán de Chuchoca hot, garnished with chopped fresh cilantro or parsley if desired.

Enjoy this hearty and comforting Chilean stew, Charquicán de Chuchoca, as a satisfying meal on its own or accompanied by crusty bread for dipping!

Pollo Arvejado

Ingredients:

- 4 chicken thighs or drumsticks, skin-on and bone-in
- Salt and pepper, to taste
- 2 tablespoons vegetable oil
- 1 onion, finely chopped
- 2 cloves garlic, minced
- 2 carrots, peeled and sliced
- 1 bell pepper, diced
- 1 can (14.5 oz) diced tomatoes
- 1 cup chicken broth
- 1 teaspoon ground cumin
- 1 teaspoon paprika
- 1 cup frozen peas
- Fresh cilantro or parsley, chopped, for garnish (optional)
- Cooked rice, for serving

Instructions:

1. Season the chicken thighs or drumsticks with salt and pepper on both sides.
2. In a large skillet or Dutch oven, heat the vegetable oil over medium-high heat. Add the chicken pieces and cook until browned on all sides, about 5-7 minutes. Remove the chicken from the skillet and set aside.
3. In the same skillet, add the chopped onion and minced garlic. Sauté until softened and fragrant, about 3-4 minutes.
4. Add the sliced carrots and diced bell pepper to the skillet. Cook for another 3-4 minutes, stirring occasionally.
5. Pour in the diced tomatoes (with their juices) and chicken broth. Stir in the ground cumin and paprika. Bring the mixture to a simmer.
6. Return the browned chicken pieces to the skillet, nestling them into the vegetable mixture. Cover and simmer over low heat for about 25-30 minutes, or until the chicken is cooked through and tender.
7. Add the frozen peas to the skillet during the last 5 minutes of cooking, stirring gently to combine.
8. Taste the sauce and adjust the seasoning with salt and pepper if needed.
9. Once the chicken is cooked and the peas are heated through, remove the skillet from the heat.

10. Serve the Pollo Arvejado hot, garnished with chopped fresh cilantro or parsley if desired. Serve with cooked rice on the side.

Enjoy this flavorful and comforting Chilean dish, Pollo Arvejado, with its tender chicken and vibrant vegetable sauce, served over a bed of fluffy rice!

Sopa de Champiñones

Ingredients:

- 1 pound (450g) mushrooms, sliced (button or cremini mushrooms work well)
- 2 tablespoons butter
- 1 onion, finely chopped
- 2 cloves garlic, minced
- 4 cups vegetable or chicken broth
- 1 cup heavy cream
- 2 tablespoons all-purpose flour
- Salt and pepper, to taste
- Fresh parsley, chopped, for garnish (optional)

Instructions:

1. In a large pot, melt the butter over medium heat. Add the chopped onion and minced garlic, and sauté until softened and fragrant, about 5 minutes.
2. Add the sliced mushrooms to the pot and cook until they release their moisture and begin to brown, about 8-10 minutes.
3. Sprinkle the flour over the mushrooms and stir to combine, cooking for another 1-2 minutes to remove the raw flour taste.
4. Slowly pour in the vegetable or chicken broth, stirring constantly to prevent lumps from forming. Bring the mixture to a simmer.
5. Once simmering, reduce the heat to low and let the soup cook for about 15-20 minutes, allowing the flavors to meld together.
6. Stir in the heavy cream and continue to simmer for another 5 minutes.
7. Season the soup with salt and pepper to taste.
8. Remove the soup from the heat and let it cool slightly before serving.
9. Garnish each serving with chopped fresh parsley, if desired.

Enjoy this creamy and flavorful Mushroom Soup as a comforting appetizer or light meal, perfect for warming up on chilly days! Serve it with crusty bread or crackers for dipping.

Berlín

Ingredients:

- 2 1/4 teaspoons (1 packet) active dry yeast
- 1/4 cup warm water (110°F/45°C)
- 3/4 cup warm milk (110°F/45°C)
- 1/4 cup granulated sugar
- 3 1/2 cups all-purpose flour
- 1 teaspoon salt
- 3 large eggs
- 1/4 cup unsalted butter, softened
- Vegetable oil, for frying
- Dulce de leche, jam, or pastry cream, for filling
- Powdered sugar, for dusting

Instructions:

1. In a small bowl, dissolve the yeast in the warm water. Let it sit for about 5 minutes, or until foamy.
2. In a large mixing bowl or the bowl of a stand mixer fitted with a dough hook attachment, combine the warm milk, granulated sugar, and dissolved yeast mixture.
3. Add half of the flour and the salt to the bowl and mix until well combined.
4. Add the eggs one at a time, mixing well after each addition.
5. Gradually add the remaining flour and mix until a soft dough forms.
6. Add the softened butter to the dough and knead until the butter is fully incorporated and the dough is smooth and elastic. This may take about 5-8 minutes by hand or 3-5 minutes with a stand mixer.
7. Place the dough in a greased bowl, cover with a clean kitchen towel or plastic wrap, and let it rise in a warm place for about 1-2 hours, or until doubled in size.
8. Once the dough has risen, punch it down and divide it into small balls, about 2 inches in diameter.
9. Place the dough balls on a lightly floured surface, cover with a clean kitchen towel, and let them rise for another 30-45 minutes.
10. In a large, deep skillet or pot, heat vegetable oil to 350°F (180°C) for frying.
11. Carefully add the risen dough balls to the hot oil in batches, frying until golden brown on all sides, about 2-3 minutes per side.

12. Remove the fried dough balls from the oil using a slotted spoon and place them on a paper towel-lined plate to drain any excess oil.
13. Once the Berlín pastries have cooled slightly, use a pastry bag fitted with a small tip to fill each pastry with dulce de leche, jam, or pastry cream.
14. Dust the filled Berlín pastries generously with powdered sugar before serving.

Enjoy these homemade Berlín pastries as a delightful treat with your choice of filling!

They're perfect for breakfast, dessert, or any time you're craving something sweet.

www.ingramcontent.com/pod-product-compliance
Lightning Source LLC
LaVergne TN
LVHW061945070526
838199LV00060B/3984